The
REMEMBERING WITH LOVE
Journal

The
Remembering
with
Love
JOURNAL

A Companion for
the First Year of
Grieving and Beyond

Elizabeth Levang, Ph.D.

Fairview Press
Minneapolis

Published by Fairview Press, 2450 Riverside Avenue, Minneapolis, MN 55454.

Fairview Press is a division of Fairview Health Services, a nonprofit, community-based health system affiliated with the University of Minnesota, providing a complete range of services, from the prevention of illness and injury to care for the most complex medical conditions.

Printed in the United States of America
ISBN 1-57749-126-2

First printing: January 2003
07 06 05 04 03   7 6 5 4 3 2 1

Cover: Laurie Ingram Design (www.laurieingramdesign.com), based on the original design for *Remembering with Love* by Circus Design

For a free catalog of Fairview Press titles, please call toll-free 1-800-544-8207. Or visit our Web site at www.fairviewpress.org.

To my daughter, Natalie,
whose life fills me with hope

CONTENTS

Three
The Uneven Path

ACKNOWLEDGMENTS

I AM ELATED TO BE ABLE TO FULFILL THE LONGSTANDING NEED for a writing companion to *Remembering with Love*. I am grateful that Lane Stiles, Director of Fairview Press, encouraged this project and brought it from concept to reality. I owe Lane enormous thanks for trusting and believing in me. He is, above all, a remarkable person of the highest integrity and ethics. I could not want more from a publisher.

In the time since *Remembering with Love* was first published, I have worked steadily to better understand the trauma of grief and loss. My learning has come in a multitude of ways and has been influenced by many wonderful people. Among them are those that have inspired me with their courage, humility, and fight: Lyle and Cindy Hilbrands, Tim, Holly, and Andrew Cashin, Sandy Maclean, Melissa Swanson, Cathi Lammert, and Fran Rybarik. There are those who have taken care of me in extraordinary ways for whom I also owe sincere thanks: Al Pesso and Diane Boyden Pesso, Mary Anders, Norma Schnoor, and Karol Dahlof.

I am quite indebted to my husband, Curt, and daughter, Natalie, who stood by me once again. They are far too accustomed to my commitment to helping others. I fear that I am not as generous and patient in return. A special thanks to my niece, Tifanne Ehrman, who despite many other obligations, was always prepared to lend a hand.

INTRODUCTION

OVER THE YEARS, I HAVE THOUGHT OFTEN OF THE PEOPLE whose personal stories are woven into the pages of *Remembering with Love: Messages of Hope for the First Year of Grieving and Beyond.* The trauma, disappointment, and pain chronicled in their stories are still very real for me. The memories often leave me in tears. I hope and pray that in the years that have passed, healing has come to these courageous people.

The Remembering with Love Journal answers a need expressed by many of these contributors—and others—for a way to record their thoughts, feelings, and experiences as they worked through their grief. As the days and weeks unfolded, they felt it would be helpful to put on paper some of their private pain. Grieving is often a lonely and frightening experience. Most of us have little idea of what to expect along the way, and we wonder what is normal, and what is not. This journal can be a companion and a guide as we travel through the grieving process. It can allow you to take your questions, worries, and concerns out of your head, heart, and soul and expose them to the sunlight. Known as catharsis, this process can be of tremendous benefit when attempting to make sense of the devastation and anguish when a loved one dies.

How To Use This Journal

Like *Remembering with Love*, this journal encourages you to go at your own pace and according to your own time clock. It is structured weekly as a way to provide some initial guidance and focus your thoughts. The journal covers fifty-nine weeks. Every page includes a theme and contains an affirmation for support and validation. There are also suggestions for reflection and journaling.

The journal is divided into five sections. It begins with "The Early Days" and is followed by "The Early Weeks." These sections explore the emotions and experiences of new grief. The next sections, "The Uneven Path" and "The Continuing Journey towards Healing," are meant to address the concerns and struggles you may have as you work to heal and survive. "Beyond the First Year" recognizes that your grief does not end at the anniversary and offers you continued support.

The Remembering with Love Journal is your personal memoir. The writing is for you, and about you. It reflects what is in your heart and soul and is an intimate expression of your journey to heal. Let the words flow uncensored and unrestrained. Let it be what it is: beautiful, raw, rambling, unstructured, horrifying, painful, vulnerable. The words you write represent your truth, what is at your full attention at the moment.

As you journal, you may have occasion to look back and reread past entries. This may help you monitor your own progress, identify patterns and themes, and guide you toward further healing.

As a writer, I know firsthand the power of putting words to paper. I trust that you will find the same sort of healing that has sustained me over the years. More than anything, I wish you peace in your journey.

The Early Days

Journal theme: *A Changed Life*

A death has occurred and everything has changed....
Life can never be the same again.
> —*from "A Death Has Occurred"*
> *by Paul Irion*

The death of a loved one abruptly changes your life. One day you and your loved one are together; the next day you are apart. The change is unfathomable. Your heart is stunned. You can't believe it has happened. Yet the change has occurred, and you can feel the dull weight of it on your soul.

Your life will never be the same. Your loved one gave your life so much meaning and purpose. Your sorrow is a tribute to this gift of love.

My loved one's life had meaning. I will let this thought guide me through the changes that death has brought.

I can write about ...

... a vivid, positive memory I have of the two of us.

... what my loved one's life meant to me.

... another time in my life when change was painful.

Journal Theme: *Feeling Unprepared*

I always knew
He would die
But not...
This moment—
Not now.

—*Ellen Olinger, in memory of
her father, Harold A. Borgh*

As brutal as it may seem, death is an inevitable part of the cycle of life. Yet death, whenever it comes, shocks and surprises us. Can we be prepared? Probably not. It is unlikely we can ever be completely ready for the finality that death represents.

In this moment, my loved one's death is incomprehensible. Still, I know that I would never feel there was a right time for my loved one to die.

I can write about ...

... a kind gesture someone made to comfort me.

... what it means to me to be prepared.

... the fears that I've felt since my loved one's death.

Journal Theme: *A Lack of Concentration*

> I just couldn't concentrate..., I felt so
> preoccupied .... like I was on automatic pilot.
> —*Juliana Ehrman, in memory of her*
> *grandmother, Katherine Immel*

Grief taxes all of your senses and sensibilities. Every part of your being is strained as you grapple with the emotional, spiritual, intellectual, and physical tumult in your life. With so much energy expended on grieving, your mind naturally loses its ability to concentrate and stay focused. You are preoccupied with your loved one's death—which is how it should be.

"Automatic pilot" allows us to make it through the day. In the short term, at least, all any of us may be able to do is just go through the motions of everyday living.

My loved one's death preoccupies my thinking and drains my energy, but I know that it is normal to feel overwhelmed by loss.

I can write about ...
> ... a specific instance of being "on automatic pilot."
> ... something I want to say to my loved one.
> ... the frustration of not being able to concentrate.

Journal Theme: *The Need to Grieve*

The minister said we should be happy…. He
told us that Heaven is more important than this
earthly life…. I felt like he was telling me I
should stop grieving.

—*Anonymous*

The belief that our loved one is in a place of glory
and eternal rest can be reassuring. Such belief can
offer us some measure of comfort and peace. Still,
we cannot deny our need to grieve and to experience all
the pain, regrets, and sorrow that accompany deep feelings
of loss.

Our loved one's existence in the world must be
recognized and celebrated, and the loss of this existence
mourned. Thoughts of eternal life alone cannot end our
grief.

**I can be grateful and happy that my loved one
is in a better place while at the same time
grieving their passing from my life.**

I can write about …
>   … a teaching from my faith about death and eternal life.
>   … my desire to know that my loved one is safe.
>   … wanting to grieve.

Journal Theme: *The Right to Grieve*

I was not the central person affected.... Yet I
felt a tremendous sense of loss. Did I have the
right to grieve his death too?
        —*Elizabeth Levang, in loving memory of
                her uncle, Tony Rizzo*

When we care for and love someone, we are
certain to feel strong emotions when that
person dies. There's no need to justify such
feelings because there are no limits or conditions on who
can grieve or how we can grieve.

We all have a right to our grief. Our feelings are our
own and are not something that can, or should, be taken
away.

**I have a right to my grief.
I cared for —and miss—this special person.**

I can write about ...
        ... a possession I have that belonged to my loved one.
        ... a strong memory I have of them.
        ... how it hurts when others ignore my pain.

Journal Theme: *Intimacy and Support*

Why is it so hard for people to touch a grieving person? Don't people know that we crave their hugs more than their words?

—*C. Renee Anderson, in loving memory of her husband, Keith*

We can sense when people are uncomfortable and apprehensive around us because we have suffered a loss. But we should not feel wounded by their discomfort and apprehension. Few people know how to extend intimacy to a grieving person.

Although hugs of genuine support and understanding can be a warm blanket of love when we are cold with grief, we should have compassion for those who are unsure how to support a grieving person.

I can gain the intimacy and comfort I need by teaching my friends and family what my needs are. I will offer hugs and trust my actions will be returned.

I can write about ...

... a hug someone gave me that showed their care and concern.

... my disappointment in those who have made little effort to console me.

Journal Theme: *The Silence of Reality*

> Mom died quietly in the hospital bed she had
> occupied for several days…. When I went back
> to the house,… I felt overwhelmed by the
> silence…. I did not know this home without
> her! The silence was unbearable.
>
> —*Leah Jones, in loving memory of*
> *her mother and best friend, Ruth*

Silence can be overwhelming when you grieve. You
hunger for the sounds of your loved one and want to
retrieve and hold dear all remnants of this special
person's existence.

At times your mind may momentarily trick you into
believing your loved one is near. Then, reality shocks you
back to the here and now. Your loved one is truly gone,
and you must rely on your recollections for comfort and
strength.

**There is an obvious silence created by my loved one's death. I
will listen to my memories to ease the reality of this silence.**

I can write about …
> … something that reminds me of my loved one.
> … what I need to fill the silence.
> … the fears I have of forgetting my loved one.

The Early Weeks

Journal Theme: *Grieving My Own Way*

Stand up tall to friends and to yourself and say,
"Don't take my grief away from me.
I deserve it, and I'm going to have it."
—*from "Don't Take My Grief Away"*
by Reverend Doug Manning

It may be hard on our friends and families when we are tearful, heartbroken, and hurting for what seems to them a long time. They want us to get better, to heal as quickly as possible.

But their timetable need not be ours, nor their understanding of grief and loss. We are each entitled to have our own grief.

**I can appreciate that my family and friends want
to see me in less pain. Still, I own my grief
and I will not let anyone take it away.**

I can write about ...

... a card or note of condolence I received that felt supportive.

... a coping strategy I am using to deal with my sadness and pain.

... my thoughts and reactions when others try to take away my grief.

Journal Theme: *Love Finds a Way*

Instructions were wired to find a beautiful smooth
stone for each missing member of the family
and place them in mother's hand one at a
time.... When conscious, she held conversations
with the person whose stone she held, or whispered
a message to be given to them. Mother died with
the smooth stones in her hands, secure in the
knowledge that all her loved ones were with her....
While our family was separated, love found a way.
—*Lila "Peggy" Azad, Ph.D.*

It can be agonizing to recall the distance that separated
us from our loved one. Had there been other options,
we would have acted on them. Instead of berating
ourselves, we can focus on the concerns and wishes we had
for our loved one. We must trust that our message of love
found its way to our loved one's heart.

**I can let go of the circumstances that kept me from my loved
one. My message of my love can be carried through to eternity.**

I can write about ...
   ... a unique object or item that I have saved in memory of
my loved one.
   ... the message of love I want my loved one to hear.
   ... the pain of missing my loved one.

The Remembering with Love Journal

Journal Theme: *Difficulty Making Decisions*

Thirty years we had been married....The mere
thought that now I had to take the reins in my
own hands was frightening.... Decisions,
decisions, everywhere.
　　　—*Meg Hale, in memory of her husband*

The burden of decision-making can overwhelm us
in the weeks and months after the death of our
loved one. We may not be accustomed to so
much responsibility, or we may feel anxious about the
consequences of our choices.

We need time to think and plan carefully. It may be
wise to seek the advice of a trusted friend or family
member.

**Although I am capable of making decisions, I can ask for help
when I need more information or another perspective.**

I can write about ...

... a friend or family member who has been a
compassionate listener and confidant.

... a decision that I have recently made and feel good
about.

... my feelings of distress over having so many decisions to
make.

Journal Theme: *Restlessness*

Sleep was a luxury that eluded me night after
night.
> —*Linda Taylor Williams, in loving
> memory of her husband*

Restlessness is a common experience following the
death of a loved one. Though we crave sleep, it
has a way of evading us time and time again.
Sleeplessness only compounds the stress that we feel
after the death of a loved one. Still, we must trust that our
body can, and will, take care of itself naturally. Over time,
sleep will return.

I will not pressure myself to sleep.
I will trust my body's natural process.

I can write about …
    … a place that I can go to that feels safe and secure.
    … a favorite bedtime ritual I enjoyed as a child.
    … the jumble of thoughts and feelings that race through
my mind as I lie in bed, trying to go to sleep.

Journal Theme: *Feelings Breaking Through*

In the days and weeks following our friend
Colleen's death, we let all the arrangements and
planning consume us ... but then one day the
dam that had been holding in our feelings broke.
—*Curt and Elizabeth Levang, in memory
of their friend, Colleen Kent*

The many tasks that must be attended to after the death of a loved one can pile high enough to temporarily block off the river of our grief. Eventually, though, this man-made dam will lose its holding power, and the intensity of our feelings will spill forth. What we soon discover is that our grief and sorrow were never far away.

**It's okay that I have been distracted. I can let my sorrow
and grief for my loved one spill out now.**

I can write about ...

... an aspect of the funeral or memorial service that was meaningful for me.

... things I do that keep me busy and distracted from my feelings of loss and grief.

... how fragile and vulnerable I feel in the aftermath of my loved one's death.

Journal Theme: *Drug and Alcohol Use*

At first, I dealt with death by repressing my feelings and trying to forget my loss. This was a mistake and caused me a multitude of problems, one of which was a serious addiction to alcohol and drugs.
—*Ken Pugh, in memory of his loved ones*

We all cope with loss differently. Numbing out the pain with drugs or alcohol is a temporary solution with illusory results. The false respite will not last long. Eventually, we must accept the truth and feel our pain.

I accept that drinking or using drugs offers only temporary relief. I will do the grieving I need to do and seek other means to support myself through this process.

I can write about ...

... a personal accomplishment that is a source of pride for me.

... some avenues of support I have for dealing with my grief.

... the mixture of emotions I feel when I think about my loved one.

Journal Theme: *Questions of Faith*

I had believed God to be a loving father. Maybe
someday I can believe in Him again.
—*Mary Van Bockern, in loving memory
of her daughter, Catherine Mary,
who died at age three*

The death of our loved one can challenge our
understanding and commitment to God. We may
feel angry, cheated, confused, bitter, helpless, and
even hopeless when we consider what has happened to us.

Suffering can test our faith and our beliefs in a loving
and just Creator. We may find ourselves for the first time
doubting or questioning God. Such thoughts are natural
and understandable.

**I can question God and my faith. I will give myself time
to sort out my thoughts and beliefs.**

I can write about ...

... someone I know who has been a wise and comforting
spiritual presence in my life.

... some of the other aspects of life that I also question
because of my loved one's death.

... the uncertainty I feel and my need for life to make sense
again.

Journal Theme: *Filling the Void*

The particular hole left by a loved one will
never be filled and we shouldn't try to fill it.
To grieve is to feel ... love ... live. Grieving is
a part of living.
>   —*Jill Cerulli, in loving memory of*
>   *her mom and dad*

Our loved one's death leaves a void in our life.
Some of us try to fill the void with whatever is
handy. Others try to pretend the void isn't there.
But the void isn't something we can fill, nor is it
something that we can ignore. Its size and shape is unique
to the loved one whose life defined it.

Rather than trying to fill the void left by our loved
one, we should accept that it is there and grieve it.
Grieving is a normal human response. We must let it take
its course, wherever that may be.

I will not attempt to fill the void in my heart.
I will let myself grieve my loved one's absence.

I can write about ...
      ... something I have done in memory of my loved one.
      ... the ways I have tried to fill the void rather than grieving.
      ... how I react when others try to censor my feelings and
emotional responses.

The Remembering with Love Journal

Journal Theme: *Accepting Reality*

Many times in those first few weeks after my
uncle's death I thought of phoning him. But
before I even had the telephone in my hand, I
would remember that he was dead.
— *Elizabeth Levang, in loving memory of*
her uncle, Tony Rizzo

Occasionally, the reality of our loved one's death
may escape us. This is natural, for we never really
expect relationships to end. But while our
memory may temporarily falter, reality quickly puts us
back on course. Like a compass, it can lead us along our
journey to a greater sense of peace and normalcy.

There may be times when I forget that my loved one has died.
I will look to reality to help me accept what is true.

I can write about ...

... a hobby or activity that my loved one and I enjoyed and
shared.

... how habit and memory can make it seem as if a loved
one is still alive.

... the sense of regret I feel that my loved one has died.

The Uneven Path

Journal Theme: *The Hurt of Remembering*

Don't try to destroy a beautiful
part of your life because
remembering hurts.
—*from "Living When A Loved One Has Died"*
by Rabbi Dr. Earl A Grollman

I t may hurt to recall the life we once shared with our
loved one. Sometimes we may even feel that the kind
of happiness we once had can never exist again. It as if
all joy is forever gone, buried in the same soil as our loved
one.

Your loved one's life is part of your life. In spite of all
that is happened, your life bears the indelible imprint of
your loved one's spirit and being.

**At times, it is painful to remember the life I shared with my
loved one. I will draw strength from knowing that
our lives are forever intertwined.**

I can write about ...

... a humorous incident or story that involved my loved one.
... an aspect of our relationship that I miss.
... my worries of never being happy again.

Journal Theme: *Special Memories and Mementos*

> My life has been filled with a storehouse of
> experiences that my Mom made possible....
> When I look back, I say, "Thanks for the
> memories, Mom."
> —*Julie Faxvog, in memory of her mother,*
> *Charlotte Margaret Joan Doherty Klug*

Many sights, sounds, and smells remind us of our loved one—the lyrics to a song, a brand of coffee, a particular flowering plant. In that pang of recognition, we often find ourselves smiling or tearing up or both.

While we may miss the life we shared with our loved one, we are grateful for the simple objects and mementos that remind us of this shared life.

I miss the familiar pattern of my loved one's life.
Today, I will think about a few of my special possessions
and the shared memories tied to them.

I can write about ...

... something ordinary that reminds me of my loved one.

... the gratitude I feel for having known my loved one.

... the anguish I feel knowing that we cannot create new memories.

Journal Theme: *Lingering Resentments*

My brother and I wanted to say or do
something special at my sister's funeral—a
prayer or testimonial. My parents asked us not
to.... I can't help but wonder if our grieving
process would have been different if we had
been allowed to share in this service.
> —*Pastor Mike Zylstra, in loving memory*
> *of his sister, Mary*

Funerals and memorial services are often a time of
significant distress for families. Working to manage
the stress and strain is honorable, but if resentment
is the result, an airing of our feelings is in order. By
expressing our feelings in a positive way we can free
ourselves from the past and move toward forgiveness.

**If I have any lingering resentments, I will tell my family.
I can choose not to harbor any bad feelings.**

I can write about ...
  ... an amusing memory of our family that makes me laugh.
  ... my need to feel understood and respected.
  ... how I feel when I'm expected to keep others happy.

Journal Theme: *Will I Survive?*

Why? Why? How can one have this much pain
and still be alive?
>   —*Joyce Barga, in loving memory of*
>   *her son, Christopher Lee*

Our loved one's death is a challenge to our will and an unwelcome invitation to doubt ourselves. Will we be able to survive? How much can we bear, and for how long?

Regrettably, there are no boundaries to our pain and no answers as to when the hurt will subside.

For now, we must take small steps, one day at a time.

No one can tell me how long this pain will last. For now, I will find others to share my burden and take a day at a time.

I can write about ...

... another time in my life when I felt scared and uncertain of my future.

... what it will mean to "survive."

... wanting to have an end to the emotional rollercoaster.

Journal Theme: *The Family's Grief*

It was rough telling the other children that their older brother was dead. They so loved and adored him.... It's been hard to deal with my grief and theirs too.

—*Anonymous*

It is tough to deal with our own feelings of vulnerability and uncertainty, much less help our friends and family, especially the children, cope with their grief at the same time.

We can set an example by our own behavior. Encouraging openness and honesty is important right now, as is respecting everyone's right to grieve in their own way. Finding ways to unify and strengthen the family will help to bring healing.

**I will model openness and honesty in my grieving
and allow my family to grieve in their own way.
I will work to strengthen my family so that we can heal.**

I can write about ...
> ... an activity or event that is a family tradition.
> ... something positive our family can do to bring us together.
> ... how tired and discouraged I feel when my family is hurting.

Journal Theme: *Life on Hold*

Joe and I had been married for quite some
time.... Now I feel like I'm alone, with little left
to look forward to. Quite honestly, I'd rather
just die too. My whole life is on hold.
>—*"Mrs. Joe," in memory of her husband*
>*and longtime companion*

When a loved one dies, the comfort and familiarity of our old life is pushed aside and replaced with feelings of loneliness and emptiness. Some of us would almost rather die than try to create a new life alone. All our dreams, hopes, and plans for the future may have evaporated with the death of our loved one. For the time being, our life seems to be on hold. While dying may sometimes appear to be an answer, more than anything we just want our old life back.

I can describe at least one aspect of my life that positively points to the future. I will focus my thoughts and energy on this positive aspect and let it help guide me to the future.

I can write about ...

... something I want to fulfill in memory of my loved one.

... a phrase or saying that inspires me and gives me a sense of hope.

... how discouraged I feel when I think about creating a new future.

The Remembering with Love Journal

Journal Theme: *Depression*

All this pain has changed my values.... All I can
think of is battling the depression and tears and
just getting through the day.
>—*Hanell Nelson, in loving memory of*
>*her daughter, Amy*

Grief can overwhelm us and deepen into
depression. Feelings of worthlessness,
hopelessness, and unrelenting sadness are
potential signs of depression. So too are major changes in
our daily routines, such as being unable to work, maintain
personal hygiene, sleep, or eat.

Sometimes, we may need professional help. Seeking help
is a sign of courage and may be the most responsible thing
we can do for ourselves and our family.

**I can monitor my emotional health for signs of depression.
I can try to change my own attitudes and thoughts,
or, if need be, seek professional help.**

I can write about ...

... *a recent event that has encouraged me and rekindled
some of my energy for life.*

... *a negative attitude or thought that keeps running
through my head.*

... *my desire to feel whole and engaged in life.*

Journal Theme: *Being Unable to Function Normally*

> My dad's death was very trying. One morning I
> went out, started up the car, and backed out only
> to hear a very loud crash.… When I glanced in
> the rearview mirror, I was shocked to see that I
> hadn't opened the garage door! I was so out of step
> with life that I didn't realize what I was doing.
> —*Suzanne Bangert, in loving memory of*
> *her father, Robert Tenner*

What is normal and routine in our lives is instantly disrupted when our loved one dies. For a time, everyday activities take a backseat to our emotions. It's as if we are disconnected from everyone and everything around us.

The shock of our loved one's death numbs us, making us feel disengaged and out of control.

I will accept that my body may not function as it usually does.
I will attempt to be patient during this period of my life.

I can write about …

… a recent situation, humorous or otherwise, that shows how out of sync my mind and body have become.

… some aspects of my life that seem to be improving.

… my distress at being disconnected and out of control.

Journal Theme: *Emptiness*

My own heartbeat sounds like
ten thousand drums
Each beat crashes in my brain
I close my eyes …
but I still see
emptiness
—*from "Untitled" by Patti Fochi,*
in memory of her son, Justin

The pain of grieving can be so loud that it sounds like the thundering beat of ten thousand drums. Yet even that great noise can echo hollow and empty inside us. We are like a lifeless shell of nothingness, empty without our loved one.

Though we know that our life must go on, our heart cannot bear such reality. To heal, we must let our heart slowly mend.

My heart is filled with emptiness at the loss of my loved one.
I will respect this pain and let my feelings be.

I can write about …
    … a pleasant memory I hold of my loved one.
    … how my loved one added meaning and purpose to my life.
    … my feelings of emptiness.

Journal Theme: *Settling Differences*

Many things, small irritations and upsets, had
existed between my mother and me for some
time. As her death was impending, we both knew
this was "it" for us.... I feel grateful for the quiet
time we had to work through our differences.
—*Al Honrath, in loving memory of his
mother, Rose Kerkvliet Honrath*

Most of us have some differences or difficulties in
our relationships with others, even with our loved
ones. Some of us are able to resolve the
differences with our loved ones while they are still alive,
and find peace. For others of us, however, this is not the
case. Our hearts ache for a reconciliation that never came.

Though our loved one has died, we can still make
amends by laying aside our differences and offering
forgiveness.

**I will create some quiet time to make peace with my loved one
and to both offer and ask for forgiveness.**

I can write about ...

... what my loved one has taught me about forgiving.

... something I have said or done in the past for which I
would like to be forgiven.

... my struggles with finding a sense of peace in my life.

The Remembering with Love Journal

Journal Theme: *Humorous Moments*

At Mom's funeral we found my son, Tommy,
only five, jumping off the table in the foyer of the
funeral home. He'd been licking shut all the
memorial cards that hadn't been used!... Now,
after some time has passed, I can laugh about
these things. At the time, though, I just couldn't.
—*Mary Laing Kingston, in loving
memory of her mother*

Humor seems out of place after the death of a
loved one. It's not that humorous situations don't
exist; it's that we dismiss them as inappropriate, or
we lack the capacity to respond to them. But with the
passage of time we may be able to look back and recall some
amusing moments. Recalling such moments, and laughing
about them, can build positive feelings to replace some of
the more painful ones that have fixed in our mind.

**I can recall some of the comical things that happened near the
time of my loved one's death. I will use these recollections to
build some positive memories and lift my spirits.**

I can write about ...
   ... one of my loved one's favorite jokes or funny stories.
   ... how awkward it felt to laugh after my loved one's death.
   ... the strain of being serious so much of the time.

The Remembering with Love Journal

Journal Theme: *Goodbyes*

That last hug …
That last goodbye
I'll treasure them always.
He wouldn't have wanted to live
in that broken body.
—*Barbara Carnes, in memory of
her father, Francis E. Sly*

Some people have a chance to say goodbye to their loved one before he or she dies. These shared thoughts and feelings may be among the most poignant and remarkable moments in their lives.

But not all of us have a last farewell. For us, goodbyes must come in other ways. We can create our own goodbye as we recall our loved one and connect with what is in our heart.

I will treasure my last goodbye to my loved one. Whether lived or created, our parting was poignant and meaningful.

I can write about …

… a time when a goodbye marked the end of a relationship.

… the bittersweet feelings I have when I think about my loved one.

… my feelings of discomfort when other things in my life draw to a close.

Journal Theme: *Fitting in Socially*

Trying to fit in is a real dilemma for me....
What am I—married or single? Where do I fit
in now?

—*Anonymous*

Knowing how we fit in socially or how to define our relationships can be confusing and hurtful after a loved one dies. If we lose a child, do we have two children or three? If a spouse dies, are we married or single? If a sister dies, are we now one of four siblings or three?

It takes time to adjust to a changed life. How best to describe ourselves may be a matter of trial and error. Voicing our concerns to an understanding friend can help us feel more comfortable about our choices.

**I will be patient with myself as I work to fit in again.
I am confident that I will soon come to know how best
to categorize myself and define my relationships.**

I can write about ...

... a group of friends I once knew and spent time with.

... my feelings of guilt when I choose not to mention my loved one's death.

... how awkward I feel when friends or family won't talk about my loved one.

The Remembering with Love Journal

Journal Theme: *Their Suffering Has Ended*

What is much too real for me is the large lump
of memories I carry in my heart of all the pain
and sickness that were so much a part of over
half of my son's life.... I am very glad that he is
free of that part of the human experience.
—*Dan J. Henderson, in loving memory of
his only child, Nathan*

For some of us, there is a sense of relief knowing that the suffering that gripped our loved one's life is finally over. As a witness to our loved one's torment and distress, we experienced our own kind of anguish. Now that the pain has ended, we can be grateful that our loved one has been set free.

I can feel thankful that my loved one's suffering has finally ended.

I can write about ...

... a time in my life when I felt thankful for a positive ending to a difficult situation.

... what my loved one might say in response to being free of pain and suffering.

... my lingering sense of anxiety and guilt over my loved one's death.

Journal Theme: *Feeling Deserted by Our Loved One*

> I don't feel like a survivor. I feel left behind.
> —*Helen Bevington, in memory of*
> *her husband*

The death of our loved one can feel like an abandonment or desertion. We had planned to be together forever, and now, suddenly, we have to go on alone.

Like it or not, we cannot change places with our loved one. Nor would our loved one want us to. We are the survivors. We owe it to our loved one to go on, if only to honor our loved one's memory. In this sense, we don't have to feel abandoned or deserted.

I can accept my status as a survivor. I will make the most of my life and honor that of my loved one.

I can write about ...

... something friends, family, or neighbors have done in honor of my loved one.

... what it means to be a survivor.

... my frustration and disappointment that life has not turned out differently.

Journal Theme: *Loss and Gain*

Vernon's death came suddenly.... As we
murmured words of hope and consolation to one
another, we knew that someone irreplaceable
among us was gone. We are less. But we are more,
too, because of Vernon and what he brought to us.
—*The staff and volunteers of Interfaith
Outreach and Community Partners,
in memory of Vernon Anderson,
coworker and friend*

O ften there is a "less and more" quality to death.
We are less because a unique person has gone
from our world. We are more because of their
rich contribution to it.

Though gone, the memory of our loved one lives on,
giving us cause to consider both the less and more of our
loved one's life and death.

**I will embrace both the less and more of my loved one's
existence. I will let my loved one's spirit live on in me.**

I can write about ...

... an important lesson I have learned from my loved one's
life.

... the anguish of knowing my loved one is gone.

... my struggles with trying to stay strong and hopeful.

Journal Theme: *Coping Strategies*

I knew I had to find a way to cope and go on.
It felt like there was an invisible door in front of
me and, if I could somehow get through it,
everything would be okay.
—*Cathy Schmidt, in loving memory of
her friend and coworker, F. Ellen Walz*

Each of us manages our grief differently. The strategies we use to cope with a loss tend to reflect our own personalities and what has worked for us in the past. While the suggestions and advice of others can be helpful, we may need to find our own pathway through our grief.

**I will rely on past experiences to help me cope with my grief.
I will survive.**

I can write about ...

... a coping strategy that I routinely rely on to give me strength and hope.

... my reactions to unsolicited advice.

... how much I want my life to be more "normal."

Journal Theme: *Our Loved Ones Together*

Our loved ones …
　　are the saints among us …
　　　　whose memory we share …
　　　　　　whose absence we mourn …
　　　　　　　　whose new life we celebrate.
　　　—*from "In Memoriam" by LaDonna Hoy*

If we are people of faith, we are comforted by the thought that those loved ones who have gone before us are together once again. And, as we remember and mourn them in the here and now, we can celebrate the new life that has come to them.

**I can be thankful that my loved ones are together.
I will let this thought bring me comfort.**

I can write about …

… a deceased family member or friend that I fondly remember and miss.

… the strength I get from my faith.

… my need for comfort and reassurance.

Journal Theme: *Fear of Additional Tragedy*

We were afraid that more tragedy would befall
us.... We became afraid of the dark, literally.
We slept with a nightlight on for over a year.
—*Steve and Mary Van Bockern*

When a loved one dies, many of us feel vulnerable and fear further tragedy. We worry that we've been singled out for disaster, and we react by trying to exert more control over our world. We want some assurance that we will not suffer further harm.

Our desire to control our world is understandable. For now, this may be how we are able to feel comfortable and safe.

**I will work to manage my fears and replace them
with feelings of safety and comfort.**

I can write about ...

... something my loved one taught me about my own inner strength.

... wanting to be safe and protected from further harm.

... my anger at having already made enough sacrifices in life.

Journal Theme: *Our Loved One's Contributions to Our Life*

Each individual is endowed with certain
instruments, and we hear the music of their
lives long after they are gone.
—*Bill Boggs, in memory of his daughter,
Anne, who was kidnapped and murdered*

T he presence of our loved one enriched our life in countless ways. As we preserve their dreams, hopes, and love, we maintain their legacy in our hearts.

I will let the unique contribution of my loved one live on in my life and in the world.

I can write about ...

... the "music" my loved one created that enriched my life.

... how lonely I sometimes feel.

... the anguish of being unable to recapture what I've lost.

Journal Theme: *Needing to Feel Close*

Sometimes I get the box with Jesse's things in it,
and I can still smell him on his little sleeper,
and I feel closer to him. I worry if it's crazy to
do this.

—*Susan Price, in memory of
her son, Jesse Lee*

There is nothing crazy about wanting to remember or feel close to a loved one who has died. In the absence of our loved one, we cling to the reminders of the life we shared. These important treasures are a way for us to keep our loved one near at hand.

**I can keep close to my loved one through the mementos
and memories I have.**

I can write about ...
    ... what I do to feel close to my loved one.
    ... wanting some assurance that what I say or do is normal.
    ... my frustration with the work of grieving.

Journal Theme: *Facing the Future*

The sound of her silk skirt has stopped.
On the marble pavement dust grows.
Her empty room is cold and still.
Fallen leaves are piled against the doors.
Longing for that lovely lady …
How can I bring my aching heart to rest?
—*from* Chinese Poems *by Han Wu-ti,*
translated by Arthur Waley

When the life of a loved one ends, it may feel as if our life has ended, too. The thought of resuming a productive and fulfilling life may be inconceivable.

Still, the responsibility for planning our future and living a meaningful life rests in our hands. The choice is ours. With an open heart, we can rebuild our life and create new possibilities.

I will take personal responsibility for my future by choosing to focus on the possibilities in life.

I can write about …

   … a choice I've made to make life more satisfying.

   … how insecure I sometimes feel about the future.

   … my reluctance to let go of the past.

Journal Theme: *Remembering Our Loved One*

So long as we live, they too shall live,
for they are now a part of us as

We remember them.
—*from "We Remember Them,"* Gates of
Prayer, Reform Judaism Prayerbook

The life of our loved one was, and always will be, part of our life. Like two tall trees whose branches intertwine, we are inseparable.

As our past merges with our present, we remember and remain steadfast in our love.

**My loved one's life is part of my life.
I will remember them always.**

I can write about ...

... an event or experience I wish I could share with my loved one.

... how my loved one continues to live on inside of me.

... how disappointed I feel when I'm the only one who mentions my loved one's name.

Journal Theme: *Accepting the Challenge*

Life can only be understood backwards; but it
must be lived forwards.
—*from* Life *by Sören Kierkegaard*

G rieving is not for the weak. It takes courage to
confront the trauma that our loved one's death
has caused us. We must be daring. To survive, we
must accept the challenge that has been presented to us.

**I can accept the challenge of grieving. I will be courageous
today and face as much of my grief as I can.**

I can write about ...

... a past accomplishment that took courage on my part.
... my willingness to take risks.
... wanting to be taken care of by others.

Journal Theme: *Looking for a Saving Grace in Our Suffering*

Lord, I know that we all go through trials. But losing my brother wasn't on my list.
—*Heidi Stallings, in loving memory of her brother, David*

It is often difficult to understand why a benevolent God would allow suffering and pain to exist in the world. After the death of a loved one, this apparent paradox can be especially troubling.

Over time, however, we may come to see some small seed of good sprouting from our loss. Though it will not eliminate our pain, it may bring a measure of consolation and peace.

I can want an answer to my suffering. I will trust that understanding will come in time.

I can write about ...
   ... a change in my life that has been positive.
   ... my inner conflict with my faith.
   ... wanting more good days than bad.

Journal Theme: *The Messages of Our Loved Ones*

All of those whose loss I have felt have left their messages. In loss I can still recount them, and in quiet space I may find other answers.
—*Colleen Kent, in loving memory of those*
she called "friend"

Our loved ones have left their marks on our lives. We find their imprints in the things they created, in the ideas they felt passionately about, and in the words they lived by.

Some of the messages our loved ones have left us may be healthy and enriching. Others, however, may be hurtful and distressing. If we feel that we have been harmed by a loved one's message, we can try now to understand it in a way that allows us to release our negative feelings.

I can revisit the messages of my loved one
and seek new understanding.

I can write about ...

... a message of encouragement that someone has recently given me.

... my irritation when coworkers ignore my need to grieve.

... how tiring it is to be in this state of grief.

Journal Theme: *Life Is Looking Up*

Surprisingly, life is looking up. I never thought
that I would see this day.… I am pulling my life
together, making right choices, consulting my
brother as I go along, and knowing he's
watching over us.
> —*Michelle Dubreuil, in memory of her*
> *friend and brother, Rich*

It can be surprising when life starts looking up. One
day we suddenly realize that the bad moments are
stretching further and further apart and that, finally,
our reservoir of strength has begun to fill again. Our grief
may not have gone away, but at least we know now that
we can survive it.

I will appreciate my newfound sense of strength.
I can be optimistic about surviving my loved one's death.

I can write about …

… a positive change in my attitude or outlook on life.

… my appreciation for family or friends that have stuck by
me.

… having some reserve strength.

Four

The Continuing Journey towards Healing

Journal Theme: *Holding On to Hope*

One must hold on to hope;
Even when the days are darkest,
The hours the longest,
When the heart aches the heaviest,
And promises that were made never come true.
—from "Hope" by Catrina Ganey,
in memory of losing a love relationship

Hope gives us strength when we are grieving. Sometimes it is the only thing that enables us to wake each day, get out of bed, put one foot in front of the other, and go about our daily activities. Hope lights our way through the dark and lonely alleyways of our grief. With hope as our companion, we will survive.

I will hold on to hope and rely on it to survive.

I can write about ...

... a recent incident or experience that has given me hope for my future.

... some good words of advice that I have received over the last few months.

Journal Theme: *"Should Haves" and Regrets*

> There were things we could have done after
> David's death, like have a special service of
> celebration. But we didn't…. Thankfully, we
> made a commitment to each other to live with
> our decisions and not regret what we should or
> could have done.
>
> —*Jim Nelson, in loving memory of*
> *his son, David*

There are many significant decisions that have to be made after a loved one dies. Yet any choice we make can be followed by a long string of "should have's" or "could have's." We must trust that we made the best choices we could, and not try to second-guess ourselves.

Regrets keep us from living in the present. For now, we must forgive ourselves and let go of our regrets.

I will let go of any regrets that I have about the choices made when my loved one died.

I can write about …

… *a good decision or choice I have made since my loved one's death.*

… *how much easier it is to forgive others than to forgive myself.*

Journal Theme: *Getting On with Life*

I am happy, and life is good; but when I sit looking through my junk drawer with all its memories, I think of how much I loved my brother and how much he meant to me. The tears come freely. I miss him.
—*Mark D. Rittmann, in loving memory of his brother and friend, Roger*

There comes a day when our grief lessens. In the absence of deep sorrow, our life may feel good again. We are healing. But the missing and yearning linger along with our happiness and never quite end.

I will let my memories of my loved one wash over me from time to time. I miss my loved one still.

I can write about ...

... a recent experience that triggered a memory of my loved one.

... my mixed feelings of sometimes wanting to move on and sometimes wanting to hang on.

Journal Theme: *New Perspectives*

I had disliked my son's friends, but after he
died, we discovered that we needed each other.
Now some of them come regularly to visit, and
we talk and play games…. How I wish my son
were here to share these times with us, to see how
my eyes have been opened to so many things.
—*Karen Grover, in loving memory of
her son, David*

Death teaches us many things, and sometimes this new learning can be very unexpected. At this point, the differences we had with our loved one can seem rather irrelevant. Change brings new perspectives, and we gain insight with the passage of time.

Though it may be sad to recall our differences with our loved one, all that is in the past. Our life has changed. With our new perspective, we see life differently.

**I am grateful for the new perspective I have gained.
I will let these new insights help me live more fully.**

I can write about …

… an unexpected change in perspective that I have gained since my loved one's death.

… my feelings of regret at not being more understanding in the past.

Journal Theme: *The Prayers of Others*

I truly believe my recovery was dependent
largely on my friends' prayers. Letter after letter
assured me, "We're praying for you."
— *Dorothy Hsu, in memory of*
her husband, Min

The prayers of our family and friends can help us heal. They reassure us that others love us, care about us, and want to help us. The prayers of family and friends give us the courage to believe that we can survive. And we are surviving.

I am grateful and appreciative that friends are praying for me.

I can write about ...

... my appreciation at receiving a card or note from a special friend.

... the difficulty I sometimes have asking for help.

Journal Theme: *Gratitude*

… I am so glad you came.
So incredibly honored
To have known you at all.
    —*from "I'm So Glad You Came" by*
Jane Peterson, in memory of her daughter,
Colleen Kryder Murphy

Whether our loved ones live for a long time or a very short time, we are honored and grateful to know them. Their presence in our life is an incredible gift. We are thankful beyond words.

I am grateful for the gift of my loved one's existence.
I will honor and remember them always.

I can write about …

… an ability or perspective of mine that I feel grateful for possessing.

… how I still feel out of control at times.

Journal Theme: *Our Loved One's Example*

My dad left me so many gifts and good
memories. He taught me to accept both love
and death through his example.
—*Dick Friberg, in memory of his father,*
Roy C. Friberg

Our loved ones are our role models, helping us learn how to handle both the hardships and the rewards of life. We are empowered by their examples, and our achievements reflect their influence. We can—and should—acknowledge the influence our loved ones have had on us.

I am proud of the influence my loved one had on me.
I will let my loved one's example continue to empower my life.

I can write about …

… an important life lesson that I learned from my loved one.

… my difficulty paying attention to my own feelings and needs.

Journal Theme: *Coming Together Again*

I found that healing is like assembling a puzzle, beginning at its center and building outward without knowledge of a border or ending. As the scene develops, the intensity softens—the healing proceeds.

—Anonymous

Our life may have felt very scattered and unconnected after our loved one died—all the pieces tiny and fragmented with no shape or form. Those early days and weeks were an agonizing struggle.

Fitting our life together again has meant facing unknowns and uncertainties. The order and meaning we have in our life today is born of hard work and effort. As we have reassembled the puzzle of our life, healing has taken place.

I can recognize the efforts I have made to rebuild and reconstruct my life. I have healed and will continue to heal.

I can write about ...

... one or two aspects of my life that feel better now and indicate to me that I am healing.

... someone who has inspired and helped me along the way.

Journal Theme: *Peacefulness*

Nothing can bring you peace but yourself.
—*Ralph Waldo Emerson*

After the death of a loved one, it can be very difficult to regain a sense of peace. We are so angry, bitter, resentful, and envious in our grief. With work and time, however, we adapt and change. We grow in acceptance and feel a greater peace in our life.

**The sense of peace I need is inside me.
As I continue to work on my grief, I will feel better
about my life and the world I am part of.**

I can write about ...

... a shift in my thinking or attitude that has helped me feel more at peace.

... how I am still working to accept my loved one's death.

Journal Theme: *Silent Remembering*

Losing my parents was devastating. Later, when
the silence allowed a small, gentle flow of music
to return to my heart, then and only then could
I experience the depth of gratitude, appreciation,
and pride for the richness of their lives.
> —*Dr. Beverly Musgrave,*
> *in loving memory of her parents,*
> *Mr. and Mrs. Fred P. Musgrave*

Our pain and sorrow can be so overwhelming that they obscure the beauty of our loved one's life. In the calm, quiet reflection that comes with the passage of time, we can rekindle fond memories of our loved one. We have much to appreciate, and celebrate.

**In the stillness of my grief I can rediscover
the beauty and richness of my loved one's life.**

I can write about ...
   ... something unique and special about my loved one.
   ... ongoing obstacles to my healing.

Five

Beyond the First Year

Journal Theme: *The Loss Experience*

Guilt:
guilt when you smile again—laugh again
guilt when you start forgetting
guilt that you have the desire to live again
guilt that you get hungry and need other people
—from "Feeling the Loss"
by Gisela Schubach, in memory
of all those who live in her thoughts

Time has marched on, and so has our grieving. We are healing, if only little by little. Some of the devastation we originally felt has subsided, yet every once in a while it crashes down upon us again full force. Is it okay to go on?

Guilt is always stalking us. But however much we may question ourselves, we must go on, if but to honor the memory of our loved one.

I can allow guilt to challenge my choices and thinking.
In the end, I will chose to go on living.

I can write about ...
... one way that I have dealt with my guilt while grieving.
... what I've learned about grief and loss from a bereaved friend or coworker.

Journal Theme: *We Never Stop Loving Them*

The best advice anyone ever gave me was to
remember that I never have to stop loving her.
—*Elizabeth Levang, dedicated to her
grandmother, Salute Belluz*

All of us experience some pressure to put the death
of our loved one behind us and get on with life.
When people admonish us that we are grieving
too long or too deeply, we feel hurt, even confused. Our
grief has no end. We will love our special person forever.
That is our right, our gift to our loved one and to
ourselves.

**I have the right to love forever.
I will never forget my loved one.**

I can write about ...
    ... a bittersweet memory I have of my loved one.
    ... a movie or book that has been especially helpful to me.

Journal Theme: *Drawing Strength*

My child was my guide in helping me grow
even stronger in my relationship with my
husband, with other people, and with myself....
So even though my child never got the chance
to grow physically, in my heart and emotions
my child is a giant and a large part of my life.
—*Lois Holmes, in loving memory of*
Baby Holmes

Our loved ones can inspire us. They can help us to live more productive and meaningful lives, to build closer relationships, and to understand ourselves better. Even in death, a loved one may open our eyes to other possibilities. The changes we make are that loved one's precious legacy.

The death of my loved one has changed me. I will draw upon my loved one's legacy of love for strength.

I can write about …
   … what I consider to be part of my loved one's legacy.
   … how comforted I feel when someone reminisces about my loved one.

Journal Theme: *Acknowledging Our Long Struggle*

We have learned what real love is about. We
have learned, too, that courage and strength can
grow as far as we are willing to allow them, and
that the human spirit has no limit.
> —*Cathy Gunning, in loving memory of*
> *her son, Freddy*

The death of our loved one has been an agonizing experience. More than once we have been anxious or fearful about our own ability to survive. Our suffering has been profound. Healing has come slowly, day by day, week by week.

Still, most of us have had some triumphs along the way. We may have come to understand what love is, what life is all about, and what the human spirit is capable of enduring. Out of our suffering new truths have been learned and wisdom gained.

**I have learned some invaluable lessons since
my loved one died. I will celebrate all I have achieved
during this long struggle.**

I can write about ...

... something I've learned about myself and others since my loved one's death.

... the worries I still have about making room for joy.

The Remembering with Love Journal

Journal Theme: *Lingering "Whys"*

I'm still trying to deal with the "whys." My
daughter's cardiologist explained to me that they
were able to learn from what happened to her
and have been able to help three other babies....
I know that someone else's baby would have
died ... but why did it have to be my Robin?
—*Diane Crater, in loving memory of her
daughter, Robin Marie Crater*

Even after much time has passed, the "whys" may
linger. Though some good may have come from our
loved one's death, it may still seem unfair. We want
answers.

Trying to understand the "whys" is natural. It is part of
the process of healing. If nothing else, it helps to have
someone who will listen sympathetically to our questions.

I can want answers to my "whys."
My questioning is a way to foster healing.

I can write about ...

... any answers I have received that have proved helpful to
me.

... how I have been able to walk through my fears.

Journal Theme: *Memories of the Heart*

We cry for all the moments
We know will never be.
Now our memories must sustain us
As your spirit is set free.
— *from "Afterthoughts of the Heart" by*
Joyce Lung and Linda Moxley, in loving
memory of Ann Marie Cavnar

Our life will never be the same. As we remember our loved one, there will always be regrets, sorrow, and a longing to have had more time. Our memories are our bond with our loved one. Though we will always grieve what we lost, we will also always remember what we shared, and in this way we will always be together.

I will allow my memories to be my continuing bond with my loved one.

I can write about ...

... my need for some alone time once in a while to take care of me.

... how I want others to remember my loved one.

THEMES

Journaling Pages

Date:

Journal theme:

Date: _____

Journal theme: _____

_____

_____

_____

_____

_____

_____

_____

_____

_____

_____

_____

_____

_____

_____

_____

_____

_____

_____

Date:

Journal theme:

Date:

Journal theme:

Date: _____

Journal theme: _____

_____

_____

_____

_____

_____

_____

_____

_____

_____

_____

_____

_____

_____

_____

_____

_____

_____

_____

_____

Date: _____

Journal theme: _____

_____

_____

_____

_____

_____

_____

_____

_____

_____

_____

_____

_____

_____

_____

_____

_____

_____

Date:

Journal theme:

Date:

Journal theme:

Date:

Journal theme:

Date:

Journal theme:

Date: _____

Journal theme: _____

_____

_____

_____

_____

_____

_____

_____

_____

_____

_____

_____

_____

_____

_____

_____

_____

_____

Date:

Journal theme:

Date: _____

Journal theme: _____

_____

_____

_____

_____

_____

_____

_____

_____

_____

_____

_____

_____

_____

_____

_____

_____

_____

_____

_____

Date:

Journal theme:

Date: _____

Journal theme: _____

_____

_____

_____

_____

_____

_____

_____

_____

_____

_____

_____

_____

_____

_____

_____

_____

_____

_____

Date: _____

Journal theme: _____

_____

_____

_____

_____

_____

_____

_____

_____

_____

_____

_____

_____

_____

_____

_____

_____

_____

Date:

Journal theme:

Date:

Journal theme:

Date: _____

Journal theme: _____

_____

_____

_____

_____

_____

_____

_____

_____

_____

_____

_____

_____

_____

_____

_____

_____

_____

_____

_____

Date: _____

Journal theme: _____

_____

_____

_____

_____

_____

_____

_____

_____

_____

_____

_____

_____

_____

_____

_____

_____

_____

_____

_____

Date: _____

Journal theme: _____

_____

_____

_____

_____

_____

_____

_____

_____

_____

_____

_____

_____

_____

_____

_____

_____

_____

_____

Date: _____

Journal theme: _____

_____

_____

_____

_____

_____

_____

_____

_____

_____

_____

_____

_____

_____

_____

_____

_____

_____

_____

Date:

Journal theme:

Date:

Journal theme:

Date:

Journal theme:

Date:

Journal theme:

Date: _____

Journal theme: _____

_____

_____

_____

_____

_____

_____

_____

_____

_____

_____

_____

_____

_____

_____

_____

_____

_____

_____

_____

_____

Date:

Journal theme:

Date: _____

Journal theme: _____

_____

_____

_____

_____

_____

_____

_____

_____

_____

_____

_____

_____

_____

_____

_____

_____

_____

_____

_____

The Remembering with Love Journal

Date:

Journal theme:

Date: _____

Journal theme: _____

_____

_____

_____

_____

_____

_____

_____

_____

_____

_____

_____

_____

_____

_____

_____

_____

_____

_____

_____

Date:

Journal theme:

Date: _____

Journal theme: _____

_____

_____

_____

_____

_____

_____

_____

_____

_____

_____

_____

_____

_____

_____

_____

_____

_____

_____

_____

_____

Date:

Journal theme:

Date:

Journal theme:

Date:

Journal theme:

Date: _____

Journal theme: _____

_____

_____

_____

_____

_____

_____

_____

_____

_____

_____

_____

_____

_____

_____

_____

_____

_____

_____

_____

Date:

Journal theme:

Date:

Journal theme:

Date:

Journal theme:

Date: _____

Journal theme: _____

_____

_____

_____

_____

_____

_____

_____

_____

_____

_____

_____

_____

_____

_____

_____

_____

_____

_____

_____

_____

_____

_____

Date:

Journal theme:

Date: _____

Journal theme: _____

_____

_____

_____

_____

_____

_____

_____

_____

_____

_____

_____

_____

_____

_____

_____

_____

_____

_____

_____

Date:

Journal theme:

Date: _____

Journal theme: _____

_____

_____

_____

_____

_____

_____

_____

_____

_____

_____

_____

_____

_____

_____

_____

_____

_____

_____

Date:

Journal theme:

Date: _____

Journal theme: _____

_____

_____

_____

_____

_____

_____

_____

_____

_____

_____

_____

_____

_____

_____

_____

_____

_____

_____

Date:

Journal theme:

Date: _____

Journal theme: _____

_____

_____

_____

_____

_____

_____

_____

_____

_____

_____

_____

_____

_____

_____

_____

_____

_____

_____

Date: _____

Journal theme: _____

_____

_____

_____

_____

_____

_____

_____

_____

_____

_____

_____

_____

_____

_____

_____

_____

_____

_____

_____

_____

_____

Date: _____

Journal theme: _____

_____

_____

_____

_____

_____

_____

_____

_____

_____

_____

_____

_____

_____

_____

_____

_____

_____

Date: _____

Journal theme: _____

_____

_____

_____

_____

_____

_____

_____

_____

_____

_____

_____

_____

_____

_____

_____

_____

Date: _____

Journal theme: _____

_____

_____

_____

_____

_____

_____

_____

_____

_____

_____

_____

_____

_____

_____

_____

_____

_____

Date:

Journal theme:

_____

_____

_____

_____

_____

_____

_____

_____

_____

_____

_____

_____

_____

_____

_____

_____

_____

_____

_____

Date:

Journal theme:

Date:

Journal theme:

_____

_____

_____

_____

_____

_____

_____

_____

_____

_____

_____

_____

_____

_____

_____

_____

_____

_____

Date:

Journal theme:

Date:

Journal theme:

Date: _____

Journal theme: _____

_____

_____

_____

_____

_____

_____

_____

_____

_____

_____

_____

_____

_____

_____

_____

_____

_____

_____

Date: _____

Journal theme: _____

_____

_____

_____

_____

_____

_____

_____

_____

_____

_____

_____

_____

_____

_____

_____

_____

_____

_____

_____

_____

Date: _____

Journal theme: _____

_____

_____

_____

_____

_____

_____

_____

_____

_____

_____

_____

_____

_____

_____

_____

_____

_____

_____

Date: _____

Journal theme: _____

_____

_____

_____

_____

_____

_____

_____

_____

_____

_____

_____

_____

_____

_____

_____

_____

_____

_____

_____

_____

Date: _____

Journal theme: _____

_____
_____
_____
_____

_____
_____
_____
_____

_____
_____
_____
_____

_____
_____
_____
_____

_____
_____
_____
_____

_____

Date:

Journal theme:

Date: _____

Journal theme: _____

_____

_____

_____

_____

_____

_____

_____

_____

_____

_____

_____

_____

_____

_____

_____

_____

_____

_____

_____

Date:

Journal theme:

Date: _____

Journal theme: _____

_____

_____

_____

_____

_____

_____

_____

_____

_____

_____

_____

_____

_____

_____

_____

_____

_____

_____

_____

_____

Date:

Journal theme:

_____

_____

_____

_____

_____

_____

_____

_____

_____

_____

_____

_____

_____

_____

_____

_____

_____

_____

Date:

Journal theme:

Date:

Journal theme: